THE
NEVERENDING
STORY

"Never give up and good luck
will find you."
—Falcor

"Kind people find out that they are cruel. Brave men discover that they are really cowards! Confronted by their true selves, most men run away screaming!"

—Engywook

"THaving a luck dragon with you is the
only way to go on a quest."
-Falcor

"We don't even care whether
or not we care."
—Morla, the Ancient One

"To the winch, wench!"
—Engywook

"Every real story
is a never ending story."
-Michael Ende

"PointlesSness is the point."
-James Hunt

Made in the USA
Monee, IL
24 November 2020

49467317R00085